First World War
and Army of Occupation
War Diary
France, Belgium and Germany

28 DIVISION
Divisional Troops
Royal Army Veterinary Corps
17 Mobile Veterinary Section
1 March 1915 - 26 September 1915

WO95/2272/8

The Naval & Military Press Ltd
www.nmarchive.com
Published in association with The National Archives

Published by

The Naval & Military Press Ltd

Unit 10 Ridgewood Industrial Park,

Uckfield, East Sussex,

TN22 5QE England

Tel: +44 (0) 1825 749494

www.naval-military-press.com

www.nmarchive.com

This diary has been reprinted in facsimile from the original. Any imperfections are inevitably reproduced and the quality may fall short of modern type and cartographic standards.

© **Crown Copyright**
Images reproduced by permission of The National Archives, London, England, 2015.

Contents

Document type	Place/Title	Date From	Date To
Heading	WO95/2272/8		
Heading	28th Division Divl Troops 17th Mobile Vety Section Mar-Sep 1915		
Heading	28th Division War Diary Of O.C. 17th M.V.S. Period From 1.3.18 To 31.3.15		
War Diary	Hagebaert St Jean	01/03/1915	31/03/1915
Heading	28th Division 17th Mobile Vety Section Vol II 1-30.4.15		
Heading	War Diary Of O.C. 17 M.V.S. Period From 1-4-15 To 30-4-15		
War Diary	Hagabaert St Jean	01/04/1915	07/04/1915
War Diary	Poperinghe	08/04/1915	30/04/1915
Heading	28th Division 17th Mobile Vety Section Vol III From 1st To 31st May 1915		
Heading	War Diary Of O.C. 17 M.V.S. From 1.5.15 To 31.5.15		
War Diary	J Of Poperinghe	01/05/1915	03/05/1915
War Diary	West Of Abeele	04/05/1915	30/05/1915
War Diary	St Laurent	21/05/1915	21/05/1915
Heading	28th Division No. 17 Mobile Vety Section Vol IV 1-30.6.15		
War Diary	Watou	01/06/1915	11/06/1915
War Diary	Westoutre	14/06/1915	30/06/1915
Miscellaneous	No. 17 M.V.S. Sick State Of Horse For Period From 28-5-15 To 3-6-15	04/06/1915	04/06/1915
Miscellaneous	No. 17 M.V.S. Sick State Of Horse For Period From 4.6.15 To 10.6.15	11/06/1915	11/06/1915
Miscellaneous	No. 17 M.V.S. Sick State Of Horse For Period From 11.6.15 To 17.6.15	18/06/1915	18/06/1915
Miscellaneous	No. 17 M.V.S. Sick State Of Horses For Period From 18.6.15 To 24.6.15	25/06/1915	25/06/1915
Heading	28th Division No. 17 Mobile Vety Section Vol V		
Heading	War Diary Of O.C. No. 17 M.V.S. From 1-7-15 To 31-7-15		
War Diary	Westoutre	01/07/1915	31/07/1915
Heading	28th Division 17th Mobile Vety Section Vol VI August 15		
Heading	War Diary Of O.C. No. 17 Mobile Veterinary Section From 1-8-15 To 31-8-15		
War Diary	Westoutre	06/08/1915	16/08/1915
Heading	28th Division No. 17 Mobile Vety Section Vol VII Sept 15		
Heading	War Diary Of O.C. No. 17 Mobile Vety Section From 1-9-15 To 30-9-15		
War Diary	Westoutre	10/09/1915	22/09/1915
War Diary	Merris	23/09/1915	26/09/1915

work/2272(8)

work/2272(8)

28TH DIVISION
DIVL TROOPS

17TH MOBILE VETY SECTION
MAR - SEP 1915

R.V.D.

28th Division.   12/4939

War Diary

of

O.C. 17th M.V.S

Period

From 1-3-15 to 31-3-15.

Army Form C. 2118.

WAR DIARY
or
INTELLIGENCE SUMMARY

(Erase heading not required.)

Instructions regarding War Diaries and Intelligence Summaries are contained in F. S. Regs., Part II. and the Staff Manual respectively. Title pages will be prepared in manuscript.

Hour, Date, Place	Summary of Events and Information	Remarks and references to Appendices
1 - 3.15. HAGEBAERT 8.45 pm St JEAN	A Staff Gale passed over this area in afternoon. enemy heavy shelling + causing damage to buildings.	Wet + cold. Heavy Thunder. H.J.T.H.
2. 3.15. 9.30 pm "	Repaired a shelter enriched by storm	H.J.T.H.
3. 3.15. 9 pm "	Nothing to record	
4. 3.15. 8-30 pm "	Section inspected by D.D.V.S. Thirty Eight sick horses admitted. Transferred fifty one sick horses to No 10 Veterinary Hospital.	H.J.T.H.
5. 3.15. 9 pm "	Nothing to record	H.J.T.H.
6. 3.15. 9 pm "	Nothing to record	
7. 3.15. 10 pm "	Nothing to record	
8. 3.15. 9.30 pm "	Nothing to record	

Army Form C. 2118.

WAR DIARY
or
INTELLIGENCE SUMMARY
(Erase heading not required.)

Instructions regarding War Diaries and Intelligence Summaries are contained in F. S. Regs., Part II. and the Staff Manual respectively. Title pages will be prepared in manuscript.

Hour, Date, Place	Summary of Events and Information	Remarks and references to Appendices
9-3-15 HAGEBAERT 9 p.m. St JEAN	Hay received is of very inferior quality	11 F.4
10-3-15 10 p.m. "	Made arrangement for bath for N.C.O.'s. Quality of hay greatly improved.	11 F.5.H.
11-3-15 10 p.m. "	Nothing to record	
12-3-15 6-30 p.m. "	Aeroplanes very active over this area	Weather greatly improved 11 F.5.H.
13-3-15 9 p.m. "	Nothing to record	
14-3-15 9-30 p.m. "	Nothing to record	
15-3-15 9 p.m. "	Nothing to record	
16-3-15 "	Nothing to record	Snow fell during evening 11 F.7.4.

Army Form C. 2118.

WAR DIARY
or
INTELLIGENCE SUMMARY

(Erase heading not required.)

Instructions regarding War Diaries and Intelligence
Summaries are contained in F. S. Regs., Part II.
and the Staff Manual respectively. Title pages
will be prepared in manuscript.

Hour, Date, Place	Summary of Events and Information	Remarks and references to Appendices
17.3.15 HAGEBAERT. ST JEAN. 10.30 pm	Nothing to record	
18.3.15- 9 pm	Admitted first case of Shrapnel wounds from 121 Battery R.G.A.	A.F.T.H.
19.3.13- 10 pm	The Section inspected by D.V.S.	A.F.T.H.
20.3.15- 10 pm	Nothing to record	
21.3.15- 8.30 pm	Received orders from A.D.V.S. 28th Divn on to transfer N° 5512 Sergt Troisington from this Section to N° 3 Vety Hospital	A.F.T.H.
22.3.15- 9 pm	Nothing to record	Strong funs westerly A.F.T.H
23.3.15- 9 pm	Nothing to record	
24.3.15-	Sent frequent ambits from Officers Enquiring for Billets for the P.P.C.L.I.	Wet & cold A.F.T.H

Army Form C. 2118.

WAR DIARY
or
INTELLIGENCE SUMMARY
(Erase heading not required.)

Instructions regarding War Diaries and Intelligence Summaries are contained in F. S. Regs., Part II. and the Staff Manual respectively. Title pages will be prepared in manuscript.

Hour, Date, Place	Summary of Events and Information	Remarks and references to Appendices
25. 3. 15. HAGEBAERT St JEAN. 5 pm	The P.P.C.L.I. are billeted in all farms etc in the immediate neighbourhood round fields &c about this farm being cut up by their traffic	Wet weather 14TH.
26. 3. 15. 8.30 pm	Nothing to record	Cold, wet am
27. 3. 15. 9 pm	Nothing to record	
28. 3. 15. 9.30 pm	Nothing to record	
29. 3. 15. 9 pm	Made payment to N.C.O's & men of the Section	14TH.
30. 3. 15. 9 pm	Enquiry from D.D.R. 2nd Army re gennel proposed for cooling	14TH.
31. 3. 15. 8 pm	Aeroplanes active in this area. & dropped bomb which exploded close to this farm about 7 a.m. No damage caused.	H.T.H.

121/5318

28.te Division

7 militärische Vorlage: Lehrin

Vol II 1 — 30.4.15.

WAR DIARY
of
O. C. 17. M.V.S.

PERIOD

From 1-4-15   To 30-4-15

Army Form C. 2118.

WAR DIARY
or
INTELLIGENCE SUMMARY
(Erase heading not required.)

Instructions regarding War Diaries and Intelligence Summaries are contained in F. S. Regs., Part II. and the Staff Manual respectively. Title pages will be prepared in manuscript.

Hour, Date, Place	Summary of Events and Information	Remarks and references to Appendices
1-4-15 HAGABEART ST JEAN. 9am	Enemy's aeroplane active in this area. Several bombs were dropped.	H/Sgt. H.
2-4-15 " 9 pm	Nothing to record	
3-4-15 " 9-20 pm "	Nothing to record	
4-4-15 " 8 pm "	Nothing to record	
5-4-15 " 9-30 pm "	Admitted Thirty four sick horses	Very wet + cold H/Sgt. H.
6-4-15 " 8 pm "	Horse shelter blown down by storm during night	H/Sgt. H.
7-4-15 " 9 pm "	Received orders from A.D.V.S. 28th Division to move horses area	Wet + windy H/Sgt. H.

Army Form C. 2118.

WAR DIARY
or
INTELLIGENCE SUMMARY

(Erase heading not required.)

Instructions regarding War Diaries and Intelligence Summaries are contained in F. S. Regs., Part II. and the Staff Manual respectively. Title pages will be prepared in manuscript.

Hour, Date, Place	Summary of Events and Information	Remarks and references to Appendices
8-4-15 POPERINGHE 7 p.m.	Left HAGABAERT ST JEAN 10 a.m. arrived new billet 10-30 a.m. New billet is situated about half a mile from POPERINGHE station on the main POPERINGHE — VLAMERTINGHE road. There is excellent accommodation for sick horses. Nothing to record.	cold weather
9-4-15 " 7-30 p.m.		
10-4-15 " 8 p.m.	D.D.V.S. 2nd Army visited section.	
11-4-15 " 9.30 p.m.	At 2 p.m. a German aeroplane passed over this area, & dropped a bomb on roof of building in which men of section are billeted, causing damage to building, but no personal hurt injured.	

1247 W 3299 200,000 (E) 8/14 J.B.C. & A.   Forms/C. 2118/11.

Army Form C. 2118.

WAR DIARY
or
INTELLIGENCE SUMMARY
(Erase heading not required.)

Instructions regarding War Diaries and Intelligence Summaries are contained in F. S. Regs., Part II. and the Staff Manual respectively. Title pages will be prepared in manuscript.

Hour, Date, Place	Summary of Events and Information	Remarks and references to Appendices
12-4-15. POPERINGHE. 6 p.m.	At 6 a.m. a German aeroplane passed over, my billet, dropping several bombs; very little damage done.	Sgt T.H.
13-4-15 — 9.30 p.m.	nothing to record	
14-4-15 — 9 p.m.	nothing to record	
15-4-15 — 9.30 p.m.	nothing to record	
16-4-15 — 8.30 p.m.	nothing to record	
17-4-15 — "	nothing to record	
18-4-15 — "	Enemy's aeroplanes very active over this area.	Fine, warm. Sgt T.H.

Army Form C. 2118.

WAR DIARY
or
INTELLIGENCE SUMMARY

(Erase heading not required.)

Instructions regarding War Diaries and Intelligence Summaries are contained in F. S. Regs., Part II. and the Staff Manual respectively. Title pages will be prepared in manuscript.

Hour, Date, Place	Summary of Events and Information	Remarks and references to Appendices
19.4.15 POPERINGHE 5.30 p.m.	Nothing to record	Weather Good. HfS.H.
20.4.15 " 9 p.m.	Nothing to record	
21.4.15 " 7 p.m.	About 7 a.m. Shells could be distinctly heard passing over this area & bursting in POPERINGHE	HfS.H.
22.4.15 " 7 p.m.	POPERINGHE being shelled.	HfS.H.
23.4.15 "	About 7.30 p.m. last night large numbers of French troops & refugees passed along POPERINGHE - VLAMERTINGE road. At 11.30 p.m. last night received order from A.D.V.S. 28ᵗʰ Division to stand by Awaiting orders. A.D.V.S. 28ᵗʰ Division notified return about 5 A.M. this morning.	Weather fine. HfS.H.

1247 W 3299 200,000 (E) 8/14 J.B.C. & A. Forms/C. 2118/11.

Army Form C. 2118.

WAR DIARY
or
INTELLIGENCE SUMMARY
(Erase heading not required.)

Instructions regarding War Diaries and Intelligence Summaries are contained in F.S. Regs., Part II. and the Staff Manual respectively. Title pages will be prepared in manuscript.

Hour, Date, Place	Summary of Events and Information	Remarks and references to Appendices
24-4-15 POPERINGHE	Shelling of POPERINGHE continues. Railhead has moved to CAESTRE. Transferred six sick horses, but was unable to transfer several, but cases owing to distance of Railhead	A/S.T.H.
25-4-15 POPERINGHE	Made arrangement with R.T.O. POPERINGHE for transference of sick horses to BASE. POPERINGHE still being shelled.	A/S.T.H.
26-4-15 "	Transferred fifteen horses from POPERINGHE Station	A/S.T.H.
27-4-15 "	Visited R.T.O. POPERINGHE who inform me it is impossible to transfer any more sick horses from the Station. D.S.V.S. instructing initial this section that in order to move back, left this farm 3.30 pm, marched to has billet - about two miles South of POPERINGHE	very fine A/S.T.H.

Army Form C. 2118.

WAR DIARY
or
INTELLIGENCE SUMMARY
(Erase heading not required.)

Instructions regarding War Diaries and Intelligence Summaries are contained in F. S. Regs., Part II. and the Staff Manual respectively. Title pages will be prepared in manuscript.

Hour, Date, Place	Summary of Events and Information	Remarks and references to Appendices
28-4-15 9 p.m.	Rode to ABEELE Station 5:30 A.M. made arrangements for transference of motive sick horses. Arranged for one N.C.O. & two men to remain at old billet, which is to be used as a collecting station for sick horses.	Fine, warm
29.4.15 9.30 p.m.	Transferred fifteen sick horses from CAESTRE Station to Base	H.Q.S.H. H.Q.S.H.
30-4-15 9 p.m.	D.D.V.S. 2nd Army visiting this Section. Made arrangements for transference of sick horses from GODEWAERSVELDE Station	H.Q.S.H.

1247 W 3299 200,000 (E) 8/14 J.B.C. & A.   Forms/C. 2118/11.

121/6439

28th Division

17th Infantry Bde: Section

Vol III

From 1st to 31st May 1915

CONFIDENTIAL

WAR DIARY

OF

O.C. 17. M.V.S.

FROM 1.5.15.   TO 30.5.15.

Army Form C. 2118.

WAR DIARY
or
INTELLIGENCE SUMMARY.
(Erase heading not required.)

Instructions regarding War Diaries and Intelligence Summaries are contained in F.S. Regs., Part II. and the Staff Manual respectively. Title pages will be prepared in manuscript.

Hour, Date, Place	Summary of Events and Information	Remarks and references to Appendices
1 – 5.15 of POPERINGHE	Transferred sick horse for GODESWAERSVELDE. Visited advanced collecting station North of POPERINGHE.	Mj TH
2 – 5 – 15 "	Visited Advanced collecting HQrs	Mj TH
3 – 5 – 15 "	Received orders for ADV. 1st Division to move SECTION to from ABEELE – STEENVORDE Road	Mj TH
4 – 5 – 15 WEST of ABEELE	Marched company from billets 10 a.m. arrived new billet 11.30 A.m. Bad water supply. Visited advanced collecting station	Mj TH
5 – 5 – 15 "	Nothing to record	Mj TH
6 – 5 – 15 "	Nothing to record	Mj TH
7 – 5 – 15 "	Admitted horses from sick horse	Mj TH

Army Form C. 2118.

WAR DIARY
or
INTELLIGENCE SUMMARY.

(Erase heading not required.)

Instructions regarding War Diaries and Intelligence Summaries are contained in F.S. Regs., Part II. and the Staff Manual respectively. Title pages will be prepared in manuscript.

Hour, Date, Place	Summary of Events and Information	Remarks and references to Appendices
19.5.15 WEST of ABEELE	Received permission to proceed to England on leave, four days	H.F.A.
24.5.15 "	Returned from leave	H.F.A.
30.5.15 "	Received orders from HDQ'RS 28 DIVISION 1st Mot. SECTION to take camp to ST LAURENT. Visited advanced dressing station.	H.F.A.
31.5.15 ST LAURENT.	Marched country from old billet 9.30 A.M. via main road ABEELE – STEENVOORDE. Arrived new billet 11.30 A.M.	H.F.A.

(9 29 6) W 4141—463 100,000 9/14 H W V Forms/C. 2118/10

121/5931.

28th ID Division

Corp hostile Felde: Sector

Bd IV 1 — 30.6.15.

Army Form C. 2118.

WAR DIARY
or
INTELLIGENCE SUMMARY.
(Erase heading not required.)

Instructions regarding War Diaries and Intelligence Summaries are contained in F. S. Regs., Part II. and the Staff Manual respectively. Title pages will be prepared in manuscript.

Hour, Date, Place		Summary of Events and Information	Remarks and references to Appendices
Watou.	1. 6. 15. 9. P.M.	Closed the advanced collecting post of 17 M.V.S.	Fine. Hot.
do	3. 6. 15. 9. P.M.	Inspected all horses 28th Divl. Signal Co.	Fine. Hot.
do	4. 6. 15. 9. P.M.	17 M.V.S. moved to WINNIZEELE area. Inspected all horses Divisional Squadron Surrey Yeomanry & of the 83rd Infantry Brigade.	
do	11. 6. 15. 9. P.M.	Returned from five days leave.	Fine. Hot.
WESTOUTRE.	14. 6. 15. 9. P.M.	Divisional H.Q. moved to WESTOUTRE. Inspected all animals 38th Field Co. R.E.	Fine. Hot.
do	17. 6. 15. 9. P.M.	Inspected all horses 28th Divisional Train.	Fine. Hot.
do	19. 6. 15. 9. P.M.	Inspected all horses A. Howitzer Battery 49th Bde R.F.A. with its Ammunition Column.	Fine. Hot.
do	20. 6. 15. 9. P.M.	17 M.V.S. moved into WESTOUTRE area.	Fine. Hot.
do	21. 6. 15. 9. P.M.	Attended parade of horses for casting by Remount Officer.	Fine. Hot.

WAR DIARY
or
INTELLIGENCE SUMMARY.

(Erase heading not required.)

Army Form C. 2118.

Hour, Date, Place		Summary of Events and Information	Remarks and references to Appendices
WESTOUTRE.	25.6.15 9.P.M.	Inspected all horses 2/1 Field D.Y.R. E and of 84? Field Ambulance.	Wet. fit.
do	26.6.15 9.P.M.	Inspected all horses 146th Bde R.F.A.	Fine. fit.
do	29.6.15 9.P.M.	Inspected all horses 3rd Bde R.F.A, went & examined these cases of this Division to M.V.S. D.D.V.S. 2nd Army visited & examined these cases & arranged for their evacuation to-morrow.	Fine. fit. Dull. fit.
do	30.6.15 9.P.M.	Inspected all horses 31st Bde R.F.A.	

WESTOUTRE.
2/7/15.

J.H.Tapley. Capt. A.V.C.
A.D.V.S. 28th Div.

No. 14. M.V.S.

Sick State of Horses for period from 28.5.15 to 3.6.15

LAST RETURN	ADMITTED SINCE	TOTAL	CURED	DIED	DESTROYED	TRANS. SICK	REMAINING	REMARKS
18.	37.	55.	-	-	1	33*	21.	*: Includes 4 Mares in foal.

(Sd) H.J.Y. Herrick.
Lieut. A.V.C.
O.C. No. 14. M.V.S.

4-6-15.

No. 14. M.V.S.

Sick State of Horses for period from 1-6-15 to 18-6-15.

LAST RETURN	ADMITTED SINCE	TOTAL	CURED	DIED	DESTROYED	TRANS. SICK.	REMAINING	REMARKS.
21.	65.	86.	2.	1º	—	50.*	33	o Pneumonia * Includes Few Mares in foal.

(Sgd) L.D. Warrick
Lieut A.V.C
O.C. No.14. M.V.S.

1-6-15.

No. 1 N. M. V. S.

Sick State of Horses for Period from 1-6-15 to 7-6-15

LAST RETURN	ADMITTED SINCE	TOTAL	CURED	DIED	DESTROYED	TRANS SICK	REMAINING	REMARKS
33.	50	83.	1	2	-	54.x	26	x. Includes 4 mares in foal & 1 mare with foal at foot.

(Sgd) A/O. J. Herrick
Lieut A.V.C.
O.C.
No. 1 N. M. V. S.

8-6-15.

No. 14. M.V.S.

Sick State of Horses for period from 18-6-15 to 25-6-15.

LAST RETURN	ADMITTED SINCE	TOTAL	CURED	DIED	DESTROYED	ABANDONED or MISSING	TRANS SICK	REMAINING	REMARKS.
26	22	48	-	1	-	4	12	31	1 Pneumonia

25-6-15.

(Sgd) A. J. Herrick
Lieut A.V.C.
O.C. No. 14. M.V.S.

No. 14. M.V.S.

A.D.V.S.
Date
28th DIVISION

28th Division

121/6306

No 17 hostile Vety. Section

CONFIDENTIAL

WAR. DIARY.

of

O. C. No 14. M.V.S.

From 1-7-15   To 31-7-15

Army Form C. 2118.

WAR DIARY
or
INTELLIGENCE SUMMARY.

(Erase heading not required.)

Instructions regarding War Diaries and Intelligence
Summaries are contained in F.S. Regs., Part II.
and the Staff Manual respectively. Title pages
will be prepared in manuscript.

Hour, Date, Place	Summary of Events and Information	Remarks and references to Appendices
1-7-15 WESTOUTRE 6 p.m.	Nothing to record	Weather fine, hot. H/F.H.
20-7-15 " 8.30 p.m.	Transferred on Lance Sergeant from this Section to No 12 Stationary Hospital	H/ F.H.
24-7-15 " 8 p.m.	Attended demonstration, on the Intra-dermal palpebral method of mallenation, by Lieut. J.T.C. Hobday A.V.C. at No 26 M.V.S.	H/F.H.
29-7-15 " 6.30 p.m.	DDVS D.A. + D.A.G. + D.D.V.S. 2nd ARMY inspected Section	H/ T.H.
31-7-15 " 6 p.m.	Considerable decrease in numbers of sick horses Admitted Evacuated by this Section during the month.	H/. T.H.

(9 29 6) W 4141—463 100,000 9/14 H W V Forms/C. 2118/10

121/1080

28th Division

17th hostile July Letter.
Vol VI

August 15

CONFIDENTIAL

WAR DIARY

OF

O.C. No 14. Mobile Veterinary Section.

From 1-8-15.   To 31-8-15

Army Form C. 2118.

WAR DIARY
or
INTELLIGENCE SUMMARY.
(*Erase heading not required.*)

Instructions regarding War Diaries and Intelligence Summaries are contained in F.S. Regs., Part II. and the Staff Manual respectively. Title pages will be prepared in manuscript.

Hour, Date, Place	Summary of Events and Information	Remarks and references to Appendices
6-8-15 WESTOUTRE	D.D.V.S. 2nd ARMY visited this section	H.f. T.H.
12-8-15 "	Major Taphy D.S.O handed over duties of A.D.V.S. 28th Division to Capt Hellard	H.f. T.H.
15-8-15 "	G.O.C. 28th Division inspected this SECTION.	H.f. T.H.
16-8-15 "	A proportion of maize is now being issued in lieu of oats for horses, and since the introduction cases of colic are becoming frequent in horses units of the 28th Division. The maize being issued to this section appears to be of an inferior quality.	H.f. T.H.

121/7707

28th Kirwin

ho 17 bestill Vety: leetin
Votum
Sept 15

Confidential

War Diary

of

O.C. No 14. Mobile. Vety. Section

From. 1-9-15   To. 30-9-15

Army Form C. 2118.

WAR DIARY
or
INTELLIGENCE SUMMARY.
(Erase heading not required.)

Instructions regarding War Diaries and Intelligence Summaries are contained in F.S. Regs., Part II. and the Staff Manual respectively. Title pages will be prepared in manuscript.

Hour, Date, Place	Summary of Events and Information	Remarks and references to Appendices
10-9-15 WESTOUTRE	17 M.V.S. inspected by D.D.V.S. 2nd ARMY.	4/T.H.
14-9-15 "	Staff Sgt. Withelman from his section, & transferred to 1/2 NORTHUMBRIAN FIELD Co. R.E.	4/T.H.
22-9-15	Received orders to move to MERRIS. Moved to new billet at MERRIS. Left BAILLEUL 10.30 A.M. VIA MONT NOIR & ST OCEAN CAPPEL. Arrived 2 p.m.	
23-9-15 MERRIS.		4/T.H.
26-9-15 "	Received orders at 6 A.M. to move station to MERVILLE. Departed 7.30 A.M. VIA VIEUX BERQUIN, NEUF BERQUIN, arriving MERVILLE 11.30 A.M. Received further orders to proceed to BETHUNE. Departed MERVILLE 3.30 p.m. arrived BETHUNE 7 p.m.	7 am, warm. 4/T.H.

www.ingramcontent.com/pod-product-compliance
Lightning Source LLC
Chambersburg PA
CBHW081248170426
43191CB00037B/2083